POLAR BEAR VS. WALRUS

BY KIERAN DOWNS

BELLWETHER MEDIA • MINNEAPOLIS, MN

Torque brims with excitement
perfect for thrill-seekers of all kinds.
Discover daring survival skills, explore
uncharted worlds, and marvel at mighty
engines and extreme sports. In *Torque* books,
anything can happen. Are you ready?

This edition first published in 2022 by Bellwether Media, Inc.

No part of this publication may be reproduced in whole or in part without written permission of the publisher. For information regarding permission, write to Bellwether Media, Inc., Attention: Permissions Department, 6012 Blue Circle Drive, Minnetonka, MN 55343.

Library of Congress Cataloging-in-Publication Data

Names: Downs, Kieran, author.
Title: Polar bear vs. walrus / by Kieran Downs.
Description: Minneapolis, MN : Bellwether Media, 2022. | Series: Torque:
    Animal battles | Includes bibliographical references and index. |
    Audience: Ages 7-12 | Audience: Grades 4-6 | Summary: "Amazing
    photography accompanies engaging information about the fighting
    abilities of polar bears and walruses. The combination of high-interest
    subject matter and light text is intended for students in grades 3
    through 7"– Provided by publisher.
Identifiers: LCCN 2021001459 (print) | LCCN 2021001460 (ebook) | ISBN
    9781644875353 (library binding) | ISBN 9781648344978 (paperback) | ISBN
    9781648344435 (ebook)
Subjects: LCSH: Polar bear–Juvenile literature. | Walrus–Juvenile
    literature.
Classification: LCC QL737.C27 D684 2022 (print) | LCC QL737.C27 (ebook) |
    DDC 599.786–dc23
LC record available at https://lccn.loc.gov/2021001459
LC ebook record available at https://lccn.loc.gov/2021001460

Editor: Rebecca Sabelko   Designer: Josh Brink

Printed in the United States of America, North Mankato, MN.

TABLE OF CONTENTS

THE COMPETITORS

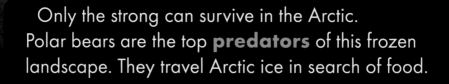

Only the strong can survive in the Arctic.
Polar bears are the top **predators** of this frozen
landscape. They travel Arctic ice in search of food.

Walruses are Arctic survivors, too. These large **mammals** can stand up to polar bears. Who would win in a fight between these two Arctic beasts?

Polar bears are strong swimmers.
Their wide paws help the bears paddle
up to 6 miles (9.7 kilometers) per hour.
Their back feet help them steer.

Polar bears are the largest bears in the world. They rise about 8 feet (2.4 meters) tall when standing on their back legs. They weigh about 1,600 pounds (726 kilograms).

These bears keep warm with a layer of fat that is 4.5 inches (11.4 centimeters) thick. Waterproof fur allows them to swim in cold water.

POLAR BEAR PROFILE

HEIGHT
ABOUT 8 FEET
(2.4 METERS)
ON BACK LEGS

8 FEET

6 FEET

4 FEET

WEIGHT
ABOUT 1,600 POUNDS
(726 KILOGRAMS)

2 FEET

HABITAT

TUNDRA   COLD OCEAN   ICE FLOES

POLAR BEAR RANGE

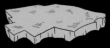 RANGE

WALRUS PROFILE

LENGTH

12 FEET
(3.7 METERS)

WEIGHT

UP TO 3,700 POUNDS
(1,678 KILOGRAMS)

0   5 FEET   10 FEET   15 FEET

HABITAT

COLD OCEAN

ICE FLOES

WALRUS RANGE

RANGE

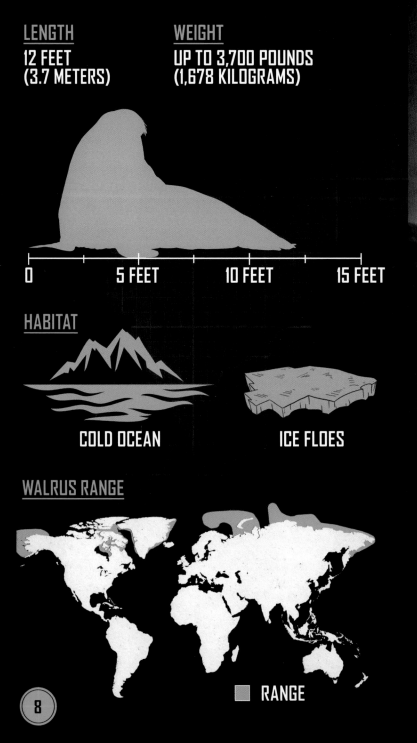

Walruses are often found lying on Arctic ice in large herds. One herd can include more than 100 walruses! These **carnivores** hunt in the water.

Walruses grow to be around 12 feet (3.7 meters) long. They weigh up to 3,700 pounds (1,678 kilograms). They have gray skin covered in short, red hairs. Whiskers stick out of their **muzzles**.

SECRET WEAPONS

Polar bear paws are up to 12 inches (30 centimeters) wide. They help polar bears walk across snow as they search for **prey**. Hair between their toes prevents slipping on ice.

WALRUS SWIM SPEED

20
10
30
0
40

22 MILES (35 KILOMETERS) PER HOUR

WALRUS

20
10
30
0
40

6 MILES (9.7 KILOMETERS) PER HOUR

HUMAN

Walruses have **flippers** instead of legs. Their flippers allow them to swim at speeds of up to 22 miles (35 kilometers) per hour. This helps walruses escape predators.

POLAR BEAR CLAW

**2 INCHES
(5 CENTIMETERS)**

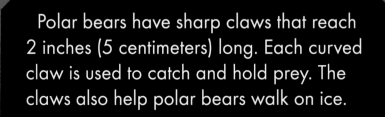

Polar bears have sharp claws that reach 2 inches (5 centimeters) long. Each curved claw is used to catch and hold prey. The claws also help polar bears walk on ice.

Walrus tusks can be up to 3 feet (1 meter) long. Walruses show off these dangerous weapons to warn predators. They also use them to jab other walruses when fighting over **mates**.

SECRET WEAPONS

WIDE PAWS

LARGE CLAWS

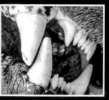
SHARP TEETH

Polar bears have 42 sharp teeth in their mouths. Their **canine teeth** cut into prey. They tear through tough **hides**. They also cause damage during fights with other bears.

WALRUS

FLIPPERS

LARGE TUSKS

THICK HIDE

Walrus hides can be up to 1.6 inches (4 centimeters) thick. Walruses also have up to 4 inches (10 centimeters) of **blubber** underneath. Many enemies cannot tear through these layers!

ATTACK MOVES

Polar bears often **stalk** their prey. Once they are close, the bears charge. They grab prey with their claws and teeth so it cannot escape.

Walruses swing their heads at their challengers. They strike with their tusks. The sharp points break the skin of most enemies.

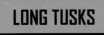

LONG TUSKS

Tusks do not stop growing throughout walruses' lives!

Once polar bears have their prey, they deliver bites to the head and neck. They bite several times to finish off prey. The bears eat their meals by biting off large chunks.

Walrus herds will circle to protect their young from attacks. They use their thick bodies to create a wall. Predators often cannot break through!

READY, FIGHT!

A hungry polar bear approaches a herd of walruses. The walruses quickly form a wall around their young. The polar bear tries to break through. It bites and claws a walrus.

But the walrus's hide is too tough. It shakes the bear off and attacks with its tusks. The wounded bear runs off. The walrus has won this round!

GLOSSARY

blubber—the layer of body fat that helps cold water animals stay warm

canine teeth—long, pointed teeth that are often the sharpest in the mouth

carnivores—animals that only eat meat

flippers—wide, flat body parts that are used for swimming

hides—the skins of animals

mammals—warm-blooded animals that have backbones and feed their young milk

mates—a pair of adult animals that produce offspring

TO LEARN MORE

AT THE LIBRARY

Murray, Julie. *Polar Bears*. Minneapolis, Minn.: Abdo Publishing, 2020.

Schuetz, Kari. *Walruses*. Minneapolis, Minn.: Bellwether Media, 2017.

Sommer, Nathan. *Grizzly Bear vs. Wolf Pack*. Minneapolis, Minn.: Bellwether Media, 2020.

ON THE WEB

FACTSURFER

Factsurfer.com gives you a safe, fun way to find more information.

1. Go to www.factsurfer.com

2. Enter "polar bear vs. walrus" into the search box and click 🔍.

3. Select your book cover to see a list of related content.

INDEX

The images in this book are reproduced through the courtesy of: Asmus Koefoed, front cover (polar bear); Egor Vlasov, front cover (walrus); Mikhail Cheremkin, pp. 2-3 (herd), 15, 20-21, 22-23; Vaclav Sebek, pp. 2-3 (walrus), 5, 20-21, 22-23; jeryltan, pp. 2-3, 20-21, 22-23 (bear); Kapitan Curtis, pp. 2-3, 20-21, 22-23 (bear body); Edwin Butter, p. 4; Jim Freeman, pp. 6-7; Zaruba Ondrej, pp. 8-9; AndreAnita, p. 10; Paul Sounders/ Getty, p. 11; Marko König/ Alamy, p. 12; Juniors Bildarchiv GmbH/ Alamy, pp. 13, 16; Igor Batenev, p. 14 (teeth); Heather M Davidson, p. 14 (paws); James_Roberts, p. 14 (large claws); Risto Raunio, p. 14; Mats Brynolf, p. 15 (tusks, hide); Hal Brindley, p. 15 (flippers); Thomas Sbampato/ Alamy, p. 17; Rhinie van Meurs, p. 18; Vladimir Melnik, p. 19.